SHOW JUMPING WITH
HARVEY SMITH

Stanley Paul, London

Acknowledgements

Stanley Paul & Co. Ltd
3 Fitzroy Square, London W1P 6JD

An imprint of the Hutchinson Publishing Group

London Melbourne Sydney Auckland
Wellington Johannesburg and agencies
throughout the world

First published 1979

© Tyne-Tees Television Limited, a member of the Trident
Group 1979

Set in Univers Light by Input Typesetting Ltd

Printed in Great Britain by The Anchor Press Ltd
and bound by Wm Brendon & Son Ltd,
both of Tiptree, Essex

British Library Cataloguing in Publication data
Smith, Harvey
　Show jumping with Harvey Smith
　1. Show jumping
　I. Title
　798'.25　　　SF295.5
ISBN 0 09 136840 5 cased
　　　0 09 136841 3 paper

I would like to thank David Jones, the producer
of the television series, for all his help in the
writing and production of this book.

Thanks are also due to Peter Greenland of
All-Sport Photographic Ltd for the instructional
pictures taken at my farm, including the
photographs of my son Robert.

The use of copyright photographs is
acknowledged as follows; Colorsport (Caroline
Bradley, Mattie Brown, David Broome, Bill
Steinkraus, walking a course); E. D. Lacey
(Raimondo d'Inzeo, Paul Schockemohle, Ted
Williams on Rival); Keystone Press Agency (Pat
Smythe, GLC Horse Show, Alwin
Schockemohle, Ted Williams on Carnaval);
Pony/Light Horse (child on donkey, child on
Shetland pony, Sally Mapleson, Graff); Findlay
Davidson (Jeff McVean); Tyne Tees Television
(pictures from the television series).

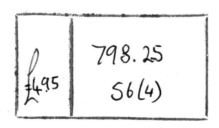

Contents

1 Show jumping – a sport for all   5

2 Getting started   9

3 Buying a suitable horse or pony   15

4 The right tack   21

5 Horse and pony care   27

6 What makes a good rider?   35

7 Schooling the show jumper   43

8 Competing at shows   53

9 All about courses   57

10 The way ahead   63

1 Show jumping - a sport for all

I've always been an animal person: always wanted dogs or horses or something like that to play with. A ball has never been enough for me. I like something that will respond ... give something back.

You only get out of show jumping what you put in. If you don't work your horse and spend the time with him, and have him understanding 100 per cent what you are doing, there is no way you can go into the ring and win classes.

He must work for you all the way up the line. You have got to half-dominate him, and he has got to trust you as well. Then you can get somewhere.

There is nothing better than getting hold of a young horse, playing with it, schooling it ... and then riding it to victory in the Foxhunter Final at Wembley. Winning the Foxhunter with a horse that you have brought up from nothing beats success in any grand prix you care to name.

In the Foxhunter, anyone — if they are good enough — can take a novice horse through the regional rounds all the way to Wembley. Age is no bar. I know of at least one rider who reached the Foxhunter Final when he was turned seventy — and he damn near won it. That's got to be lovely for the sport.

If I had my life over again there's not a great deal I would change, because show jumping has taken me all round the world. I enjoy playing with horses and the open-air life and the only time I get bored is when I'm sat at home doing nothing — though that doesn't happen a lot.

You have got to be willing to put in a lot of time if you want success. Often at the end of a long day competing I have to set off immediately on a long drive home and quickly turn my thoughts to the things I've got to do the following day.

Show jumping has something for all the family. The mums and dads and the kids and the grandparents can all get involved. I tried hard to make this clear in my series for Tyne Tees Television, and I had in my class a novice rider in his forties. He was a former miner; until he got involved with horses through his wife starting to ride, he thought show jumping was only for cissies. He soon changed his mind and, if you watched the programmes, you will know that he had a lot of fun when we got him jumping higher than he had ever gone before.

Ronnie Massarella, Chef d'Équipe to the British international team, reckons that Britain produces great show jumpers because the competitors come from all walks of life. Sure; there is a great cross-section. A bit different from when I began and most of the people running it seemed to be brigadiers and colonels.

It seems strange when I recall that my first horse cost £33 and my first wagon £50. At one time my brother, John, and myself used to get to gymkhanas by borrowing the wagon my father used for transporting men in his building business. We converted it by putting a couple of old doors at the back and stretching a cover over the top. Ask people to do that today and they would go crazy.

I'm sure no other sport can match the comradeship you get in show jumping. Inside the show ring, jumpers fight tooth and nail for success, but outside the ring they are the finest bunch of people you will ever meet.

Unlike a lot of other sports, if you don't win at show jumping there is no financial reward. You have got to be trying your best all the time. You can get away with being a bit off colour if you

It takes a lot of dedication and determination to become a champion, and no one displays these qualities better than Caroline Bradley, seen here on Sandyman during the British National Championships at Hickstead, 1975

play for a cricket or football team, but not in show jumping. And don't forget, a show jumper has to pay to compete, and there is no guarantee that he will get any return.

It is one of the fairest sports in the world. You cannot cheat and that, in my book, is why the Russians are no good at it.

Sure, show jumping has rewarded me handsomely, but to me success does not mean money and things laid out about you. Success is the sense of achievement I feel when I get to a show with a horse and we do a really good job and win. That is better than anything that money can give you.

There is no one more dedicated than Caroline Bradley, and I often pull her leg and say that if someone put on a show at the North Pole on Christmas Day, and the prize money was only a fiver, she would be there. But that is the sort of dedication you have got to have to succeed at show jumping, and you will find all the top riders have it. If not, they don't stay at the top long.

And we don't have any hang-ups about the difference between men and women. It is how good a jockey you are — not whether you are a man or a woman. It is how well you understand your horse to get the best out of him that counts most.

A little girl cannot play soccer or cricket with the lad next door, but she can take him on and beat him at show jumping. It is much easier to get girls to ride than boys and I reckon that, for girls, ponies are a natural step on from looking after dolls. Girls love to pamper and pet their ponies and comb them and love them, but most boys prefer the sort of communication they get through training with other lads in a soccer or cricket team.

You have to be a bit of a loner to get on at show jumping, for the secret is the number of hours you put in working with your pony or horse. It is like the long-distance runner. He is out on his own, and I like that; it gives me a lot of satisfaction. But then I have always been a bit of a loner and I think my youngest lad, Steven, is the same.

It does not matter what age you are when you start show jumping. It's the amount of time you spend on the horse's back. Just look at the number of people who start driving a car in their forties and fifties when they can at last afford it. You wouldn't argue that because they are late starters they cannot become competent drivers, and it's the same with show jumping. If you are prepared to spend the right amount of time on the horse's back and get your balance right then it will work out right.

Maybe to start with you will jog up and down like a jelly and think, 'Oh, dear! I'll never do this,' but if you put in the hours on the horse it will all slip into place and you will be sitting there, pulling all the levers and doing everything naturally.

You do not have to be rich to be a show jumper. I will explain as we go on how you can get started if you cannot afford a horse, though there is nothing like owning your own animal.

No doubt a lot of people who watch me on television wish they could take up show jumping but think they are not fit enough and possibly past it. Sure, there are jockeys who spend a lot of time working on their fitness, using all kinds of exercises, but others who couldn't run one hundred yards to save their lives achieve a lot of success because they have a natural feel for a horse.

The greatest satisfaction I get out of show jumping comes when I've had an unbeatable round: when the horse has been working 100 per cent for me — really firing and really jumping and no matter where I have put him he was bound to jump the fence.

Those moments are especially satisfying when it's a horse that I have managed to get without paying out a lot of money, and then worked him up to the right pitch. That's real satisfaction. And maybe I have beaten other riders who have spent £60,000, £70,000 or even £80,000 on a horse.

Different horses suit different people. A horse can be absolutely useless with one rider, then change hands and within a month be a super horse. It's like a marriage to me. If it works it's great. If it doesn't it's a disaster.

To make the most of show jumping never forget that there is no substitute for miles on the clock . . . getting the right feel for the job

and a good relationship with your horse through spending hours on his back.

The perfect rider should have the balance of a ballerina, the eye of a hawk, the hands of a pianist and the legs of a blacksmith.

If you are a beginner pick yourself one or two model riders from among the big winners and watch closely how they do it. Study them in action as often as possible and get to know the little movements and flaws in their make-up. In this way you will learn as much as a teacher can drill into you in twenty years.

That great Englishwoman Pat Smythe and the beautifully balanced and relaxed Raimondo d'Inzeo, from Italy, were the heroes on whom I based my style.

Pat had a wonderful, bouncy way of going . . . like a golf ball when it lands on hard ground. She always had a horse balanced on the bridle so that she could jump from any stride. She did not ride with as much leg as Raimondo, and that could have let her down at times. But her

Beginners should study the top riders in action as often as possible. I based my style on two great competitors – Pat Smythe and Raimondo d'Inzeo – because of their wonderful bouncy way of going. Capt. Raimondo d'Inzeo on Bowjack competing in the Nations Cup at the Royal International Horse Show, Wembley 1968

determination and cool thinking made her a superb competitor. *My, she was cool!*

Pat has retired from show jumping, but Raimondo continues to be a star, riding as relaxed as ever and now well into his fifties. Like Pat, he has a bouncy way of riding and the fact that he is still around at the top after so many years proves that his style takes little out of him. Raimondo rides in a way that just makes horses want to run and jump.

He is also one of the finest jockeys in the world at coaxing the best out of a bad horse. Raimondo has not had a fortune spent on his horses like a lot of riders yet he has consistently stayed at the top.

7

2 Getting started

I imagine that few of you have the cash handy to go straight out and buy a horse. In any case, it is always wise to see if you like show jumping before committing yourself to a lot of expense.

There are plenty of riding schools, and a glance in the Yellow Pages should tell you what you have in your immediate area, but it will be worth your time to shop around first.

Bob Stoker, who runs the riding school at Stannington near Newcastle where we made the television series, believes that the ideal instructor should be warm and encouraging and should do nothing to upset a new rider or make them feel inferior.

For those beginners who are a little bit afraid of making fools of themselves at the start, instructors give private lessons so that they can get the hang of things before joining a class. You can also borrow a riding hat from the tack room at the school so that you need spend only the cost of the first lesson before making up your mind whether you want to go on.

This is very useful for those parents who get bitten by the bug themselves after finding the money for their children to take up riding. With two or more riders in the family the cost will soon mount up.

If the riding school is a good one, there is also a wonderful spirit of comradeship amongst the members and plenty of opportunity for you to talk your problems over with other riders who have had similar experiences. This is important to the shy beginner.

It is also worth bearing in mind that not everyone wants to go on and compete in the big show rings; for many the fun they get through belonging to the local riding school and entering small area jumping shows is quite enough.

Pat Smythe on Mr Pollard at the Royal International Horse Show, White City 1958

Schools also hold small shows all the year round, with fences at a modest height to help the jockey build up confidence. In the beginning every rider completing a clear round receives a rosette, and when riders are more experienced some competitions have a jump-off against the clock. However, jumping against the clock is not to be encouraged at this stage. It might be exciting for spectators, but it is not good for a horse when a novice rider kicks and pulls it about to hurry it out of its stride. Also it is far more important for the beginner to master the right technique before worrying about speed.

If you are lucky enough to own your own pony or horse you can usually enter the small shows run by riding schools, but some school shows are run exclusively by and for the clients.

When you have made up your mind that you like riding, the necessary clothing need not, in the beginning, cost a fortune, but whatever you do never get up on a horse without a riding hat that fits properly. If you go out without the correct headgear then — like the motor-cyclist who forgets his crash helmet — you are taking a foolish risk and could well pay dearly for it. Riders who lose their headgear while riding in a British Show Jumping Association (BSJA) competition are quite rightly fined. It is not a dangerous sport, but it can so easily become one if you do not follow the rules.

I also believe that a pair of good boots are essential: poor quality or the wrong sort of footwear can easily get caught up in a stirrup so you are dragged along. If you are not doing a lot of riding there are some reasonable rubber riding boots on the market, but it is worth the extra cash to get a good pair of leather boots.

You can make do with a pair of jeans instead of riding breeches and maybe a sweater at the

start, but once you compete at a BSJA affiliated show you will need to follow the association's rules on dress.

Never go out riding without wearing the correct headgear. Show jumping is not a dangerous sport – but it can become one if you do not follow the rules

Choosing a suitable pony

Today my two sons, Robert and Steven, are both very competitive young horsemen, but like a lot of parents I was too ambitious when they began riding; I think that I went close to putting them off show jumping altogether. I suppose with my experience I should have known better, but I was so determined to make them the greatest jockeys in the world.

Robert was about seven and Steven six when I bought some 13.2 hh ponies which were far too big for them; after messing about for six months they were both very unhappy and I eventually tumbled to the fact that I would have to go back a stage.

Taking the advice of a friend, I bought a donkey and it worked a treat. It was slow and docile; they could get on it knowing they would not hurt themselves. Even on the occasions when they did use their stick too much – as excited youngsters are bound to do – the donkey would only jog along a little faster. It was just the job.

After that I let them have a little black and white Shetland pony and a cowboy saddle and they thoroughly enjoyed themselves, flying all over the place, thinking they were Roy Rogers and Tom Mix. That was great.

The Shetland was that little stage on from the donkey and would not harm a fly.

They did not jump at that time, but they were already putting those miles on the clock that are essential if a rider is to get the right feel and balance. If a rider does not feel safe walking or trotting down a road there is no way he can feel confident going to a jump.

A donkey is ideal for introducing youngsters to riding. Then, like my boys, they could progress to a Shetland pony

Too many parents over-face youngsters by putting them on animals that are far too big. A pony that is a little too small for the child is better because then, at least, the rider is always boss of the situation. It is also worth bearing in mind that if horses or ponies are over-fed they get very frisky and can easily make fools of the youngsters, especially if the horse is too big for the rider.

I cannot over-emphasize that you should not push children too quickly at the start. It could put them off riding for ever. The jockey must always be in command of the situation.

Ponies are divided into two classes by the British Show Jumping Association, according to their total winnings. Until they have collected £74 in prizes they are Grade JC and after that they are Grade JA, and should have plenty of experience. So I believe an old JA pony who knows his way around is best for a youngster starting show jumping.

Just as with people, you meet good and bad characters among horses and ponies, and the young novice rider should, ideally, get the feel of things with an old docile pony that can teach the rider something.

Just in case you are not aware of it, a horse's height is measured in hands, the hand being four inches, based on the old method of placing one flat hand on top of another up the front leg to the withers.

The smallest pony in BSJA competitions is 12.2 hh and the highest is 14.2 hh; though clearly a lot depends on the size of the youngster, a rough guide is: a 12.2 pony until the child is seven, possibly eight; a 13.2 pony until they are about ten, and after that a 14.2 pony.

The pony, Deansgrove, ridden by Gillian Greenwood in the television series, is a good example of how a well-behaved, experienced animal can help a rider learn the sport with con-

11

An experienced pony can teach a beginner a great deal. Deansgrove, ridden by Gillian Greenwood in the television series and seen here on the extreme left, could go round on his own if he could read the numbers

Graduating to horses

fidence. When I bought him in Dublin I wasn't really in the market for a pony, but the man who persuaded me to take him did me a favour. He was right when he said he was an angel and that I would not regret buying him. If Deansgrove could read numbers he could go round on his own. He has taught all the youngsters who've been on his back how to win first-place rosettes.

But parents must remember, when a child has gained enough experience they should pass on that kind of pony to help another beginner.

A good many parents also forget that when switching from ponies to adult competition youngsters still need to start with an animal who knows the job.

As I have already mentioned, novice horses and novice riders do not go together. The rider moving on from JA ponies should buy an experienced horse to begin with, because it takes a lot of skill and hard work to succeed with a young, green horse.

In adult competitions the BSJA put horses into three divisions: Grade A for those who have won £400 and over; Grade B with winnings between £150 and £399; Grade C, from nothing to £149.

The long and the short of it at the 1975 Greater London Horse Show, Clapham Common. Can you spot the mistake? The girl on the horse should be wearing a hat!

3 Buying a suitable horse or pony

When you buy your first horse or pony get one that has been doing the job you want it to do. Never pair a novice animal with an inexperienced rider. The new rider must have a horse or pony that knows its way around, and that applies whatever your age.

The German international Paul Schockemohle is a perfect example of how a rider can get a grasp of show jumping through the know-how of old, experienced horses.

When he started he was so awkward his big brother Alwin often urged him to pack it in for fear that he would harm himself. But Paul was very determined, and he bought some old grade A horses that were supposed to be finished and then practised and practised until he came good.

Remember the old saying when you go out to buy a horse: let your eyes be your judge, your pocket your guide — and your money the last thing you part with.

You only buy right horses off right people, and you should never buy in a hurry. It is surprising the number of people who fly in and buy an animal without finding out whether it is exactly what they want and — just as important — whether it fits their pocket. If ever I get desperate and rush out and buy a horse you can usually bet on me picking a wrong 'un.

Buying in a panic is the difference between being on a hot favourite and backing a 50-1 long shot.

Get advice from an expert. Presumably, if you are thinking about buying a horse or pony for show jumping you will have had basic instruc-

The style of an international — Paul Schockemohle from Germany riding Abadir, Hickstead 1973. Paul is a perfect example of how a rider can get a grasp of show jumping through the know-how of old, experienced horses

tion at a riding school and will have met people who know what they are talking about. In any case, there are always plenty of old horsemen about who are willing to help you.

Personally, I believe you should be very wary of horse sales; though saying that will no doubt upset a few people. I am not suggesting that all sales are wrong — far from it — but if you do not know what you are looking for you can easily buy a horse in a sale that will run off every time you get on him. People get rid of their rubbish in sales and it's easy to buy a horse with a defect.

I have bought good horses in sales, but after years of experience I know what I am looking for. I certainly make sure that I find out the form and past history of an animal before I buy. If a horse does not have a warranty it could be lame, or you could get home and find that underneath a long mane it has an eye missing.

There are villain horses like there are villains among the people you meet. A horse is not born that way — it could have been made bad by the way it has been treated.

The safest course, if you are looking for a child's first pony and see one advertised in the local newspaper, is to get a recommendation from someone who knows showjumpers. Then you can see the kind of people who own the pony you are after, and the children who have been riding it. And, most important, you can see what it has done for them.

If all that makes sense, get the vet to look it over so that you have taken every precaution possible.

I made an interesting deal at the Dublin Horse Show in the mid sixties when I bought Mattie Brown.

He was warming up for an event when I spotted him and he sailed over his practice fence, obviously determined not to touch it. Then he gave me a big wink as he came past.

A tense moment for myself and Mattie Brown during the Nations Cup at Hickstead in 1971. My partnership with Mattie Brown was the result of an interesting bargain struck at the Dublin Horse Show

A nice, stockily built horse, he looked just right for me and he was alert and sharp in everything he did.

In the ring he galloped through the start and stopped at the first fence three times, making me think to myself: 'Well, you're on my side old lad. You're trying to help me buy you.'

Afterwards as owner and rider were having a lively inquest I butted in to inquire if the horse was for sale ... a silly thing to ask in Dublin where every horse is for sale.

'Sure, he's for sale – at £25,000,' said the owner. But in the next breath he came down to £10,000 so I decided to hang on for a bit.

After haggling over the price all day I became determined to make a deal.

'Be sensible, Paddy, how much for the horse?' I asked yet again.

'I'll have to take £4000,' he said. 'I couldn't go home and let the neighbours know I'd taken less.'

I suggested that I make out two cheques. One for £4000 which he couldn't cash, but could show the neighbours and another for £2000 which he could put in the bank – and he accepted my offer.

Make sure when you buy a horse for jumping that he has a big, bold eye ... an indication that he will be brave. A lot of good, intelligent horses also have two or three wrinkles above each eye which suggests to me that they will do some worrying for the rider.

Also look for a horse with a fine broad outlook – good broad head – and though it may sound silly, I also believe that horses with a couple of 'dimples' formed by the skin just above the eyes have something special about them ... that they are genuine animals.

Then, when you stand back and look at him sideways on, you should get an impression of an upstanding, big, powerful animal. Anyone who has been knocking about with horses for a while will tell you that it is possible to feel whether a horse has the right conformation.

The neck needs to be turned over beautifully at the top: a horse with a U neck is a star-gazer

As well as a fine, broad outlook, the genuine jumper will have a couple of dimples just above the eye

Look for a big, bold eye and a few wrinkles if you want an ideal jumper who takes his job seriously

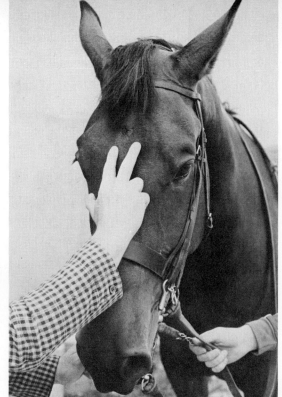

The neck should be turned over at the top

The 'look' of a jumper — upstanding, big, powerful. An experienced horseman can feel whether a horse has the right conformation

and, because he has his nose stuck in the air, he cannot see where he is going.

After that, look for a strong, deep shoulder, sloping at nearly forty-five degrees from the withers to the front of the chest. Horses with shoulders that are set very nearly straight up and down do not make good jumpers, and horses with short, stubby shoulders can't run and bend their knees properly.

Because show jumping is an explosive event you want a deep-bodied horse, built on short legs so that when you look down the legs his knees seem to be nearly on the floor. That way all his limbs will be short and powerful.

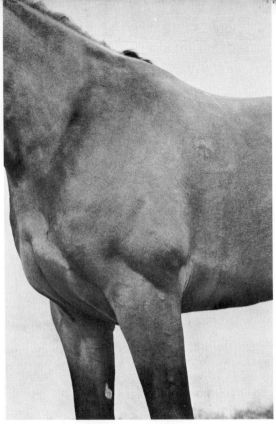

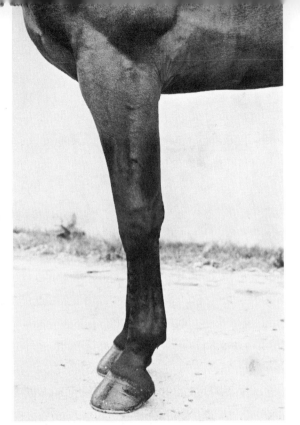

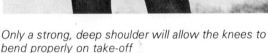

Only a strong, deep shoulder will allow the knees to bend properly on take-off

The limbs should be short and powerful. When you look down at a horse's legs the knees should appear to be nearly on the floor

A horse should have a good middle – not tucked up so that the belly touches the backbone – and strong loins are most important

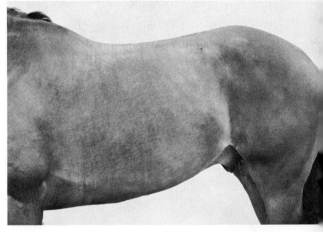

Some like horses with really short backs, but I fear that can restrict their scope when jumping. On the other hand, I try to avoid horses with really long backs, the sort that look as if they could accommodate two saddles.

I prefer a horse with a good middle – not tucked up so that his belly is touching his backbone – and then, most important, he must have strong loins. Nine times out of ten, good jumpers slope down from the top of the rump to the tail, but really it is down in the second thigh that they want to be big and strong; so that when looked at from the rear the backside appears to be thicker at the bottom than at the top.

You must be absolutely sure that the horse has a good pair of hocks because this is where all the power comes from to get you off the floor, and so much can go wrong with them. The hocks – like the knees – should be built close to the ground.

It is a habit of mine when buying a horse to tap the shins lightly with the side of my foot to see how they will react when they rap the poles. A horse that doesn't mind hitting poles will clearly never make a show jumper.

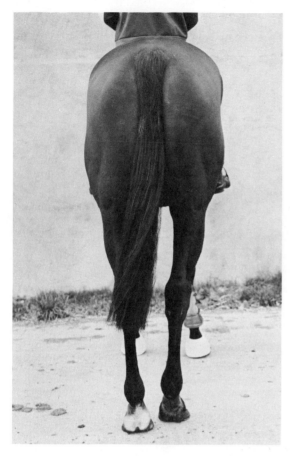

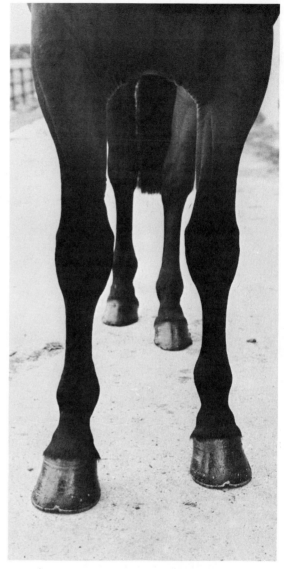

A lot depends on how well built your horse is in the second thigh. If he's the right shape the backside will appear thicker at the bottom than at the top

A fine set of feet are vital to help a horse cope with the tremendous strain when he lands after clearing a fence

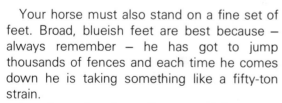

Your horse must also stand on a fine set of feet. Broad, blueish feet are best because — always remember — he has got to jump thousands of fences and each time he comes down he is taking something like a fifty-ton strain.

I prefer to buy four-, five- or even six-year-olds, though you cannot do a lot of jumping with them at that age. Like a young apprentice who has not long left school they soon get tired and cannot do a full day's work. A four-year-old might come out for a session kicking and gay but twenty minutes later he will be shattered.

A five-year-old who has been out hunting and put some miles on the clock is perhaps a better bet than a green four-year-old just off the farm, because the older horse will have been pulled and towed about and he will have had a saddle on his back and a bit in his mouth many times. He should also have a natural jump and when he goes down to a fence, he will snap his knees because there is no way he wants to hit it.

I won't attempt to talk about the price of horses here because it is constantly changing.

Right: *The ideal bridle for beginners — the snaffle with a cavesson noseband which goes above the bit. If you can put three fingers between the strap and the head, it's not too tight*

A simple, jointed bit

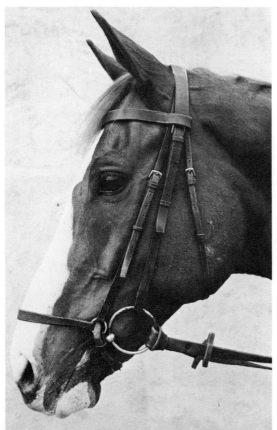

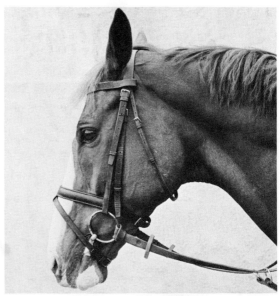

A cross nose-band — a compromise for the horse that doesn't pay attention quite enough

Left: *The drop noseband is best for controlling the horse who is more concerned with fighting his rider than getting on with the job*

4 The right tack

Bridles

In my book, the ideal bridle for beginners — and certainly the most popular — is the snaffle, using a cavesson noseband and a simple, jointed bit, which carries the least threat to the horse's mouth when the novice loses control.

The noseband is there to prevent the horse opening his mouth and putting his tongue over the bit, so if it is slack he will be too busy larking about with his tongue to concentrate on what he is doing — and that way he is bound to hit fences.

Because some horses respect things and others don't, there are three types of noseband.

The cavesson, above the bit, is the least severe. The sensitive horse will work all day with a cavesson noseband, but the wooden-head who is more concerned with fighting his rider than getting on with the job will need a drop noseband which fits below the bit on the most sensitive part of the nose. You must be careful, then, to make sure that the drop noseband is put on well clear of the nostrils. Between these two is the cross noseband, which comes together at the front of the head.

I like a noseband to fit fairly tight. Some like them loose, but if — once you have tightened the strap up — you can put three fingers between the strap and the head it should be all right. He can still play with his bit, and you can give him lumps of sugar and make a fuss of him.

When you put the bridle on, slip your thumb carefully into his mouth so that he opens up for you to slip the bit in and pull it up. The best man I ever saw putting a bridle on a horse was a fellow called Len Carter. His hand was just like a piece of silk going over the horse's head.

After putting on the bridle make sure that it fits comfortably, and that his mane is not trapped at the top of the head. Everything should be nice and easy, and fit as comfortably as a pair of shoes. If a horse's bridle is nipping him he will start shaking his head and he will not want to know about you because he is thinking of the discomfort with his ears and head.

Wherever I travel I take a large bag containing dozens of different bits, and there is not a horse in the world I cannot fix up from that bag, but I try to stick to the snaffle. Only when I have a complicated horse do I dive into my bag of many bits, and this is not something that I recommend to the novice. You can so easily damage a horse's mouth if you get the wrong bit and, in any case, the simple ways are best in show jumping.

You may need to use a more complicated bit, if for example, the horse is too strong and not obedient quickly enough, but whatever you do, first seek guidance from someone who knows what they are doing.

The best advice of all, though, is to get a horse with a nice snaffle mouth that you can feel when you ride. The last thing the average rider wants is a complicated horse.

It's not a bad idea for a novice to have a neck-strap. (See photograph on page 24). Many beginners fear that if something goes wrong they have nothing to grab; a neckstrap will solve this and prevent the jockey catching hold of the horse's mouth.

Martingales

To help keep the horse obedient I like a running martingale. It will also save you from having your teeth knocked out through him throwing his head back unexpectedly.

At one end of the running martingale are two rings through which you pass the reins; the other end is attached to the girth under the horse's belly.

I ride in competitions with a running martingale to keep a horse steady if he is inclined to

Above: *The running martingale attached at one end to the reins and at the other end to the girth*

The standing martingale straps a horse's head down and is strongly criticized in some quarters

throw his head back. Also, I have some horses who lean on the rings and that gives them more distance over combinations.

There are strong arguments against the use of the standing martingale, which literally straps the horse's head down. I never use them myself, but they can be useful when getting youngsters started or to help correct a horse that has been badly trained. My youngest son, Steven, rides particularly well with one.

The standing martingale is a strap fixed at one end to the cavesson noseband and at the other end to the girth under the horse's belly.

I read somewhere that it was first introduced to help a rider with a poor seat who was inclined to hang on to the horse's mouth and in so doing made him into a star-gazer.

In my lad's case, it helps cover up some little mistakes he makes, for example, when he has a pull at a horse's mouth at the wrong time.

When you are interested in going out and winning, little things like that can be important, but there is — I agree — a lot to be said for the argument that it is a lazy way of training a horse, and that a jockey should learn how to get a horse's head down without a device like this.

I use draw reins in training — from the hands, through the snaffle bit and down through the horse's legs to the girth under the belly. A breastplate is attached to the saddle to make sure that it stays in place. Also note the neckstrap — useful for beginners as it provides something to grab in case of mishaps

In BSJA competitions a standing martingale may be attached only to the cavesson noseband, fitted above the bit. Never put it on a dropped noseband because that could cause the horse severe pain.

Most show jumpers like to use draw reins when training their horses, but they are not permitted in BSJA competitions. I use them like the Germans do, from my hands, through the snaffle bit and down through his legs to the girth under the belly. That way you have a two-to-one pulley which doesn't restrict the horse in any way, but at the same time keeps his head in the right position when you go into a fence, so he cannot throw his head up and look anywhere, or back at you.

Saddles

I like to sit down into a saddle as the cowboys do, and I find that a short saddle with a good padded knee roll suits me best.

It is always worth paying for a well-made saddle in very soft leather so that you can feel the horse between your legs. You will never

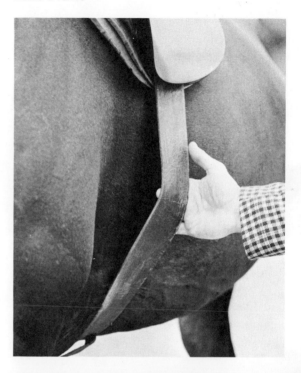

Buffalo hide is ideal for the girth because it will stretch a little when the horse becomes tense as he clears a fence

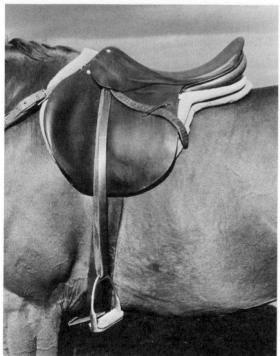

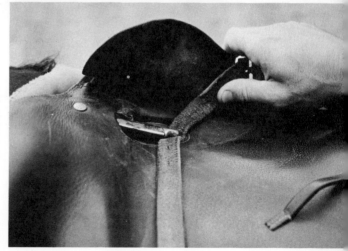

Regular checks should be carried out to make sure that the saddle safety bars — essential for children — are in perfect working order

You'll never regret paying a little extra for a well-made saddle. I prefer a short saddle with a well-padded knee roll

23

Stirrup safety irons have one side of the iron replaced by a rubber band and are an essential precaution for the young or inexperienced rider. They are always used by Catherine Emsley (left on Midget Gem) and Gillian Greenwood (on Deansgrove) who took part in the television series

Always make sure your horse's legs are protected by tendon boots (or bandages) and his feet by over-reach boots when he is jumping. Otherwise he could easily damage himself, especially when landing

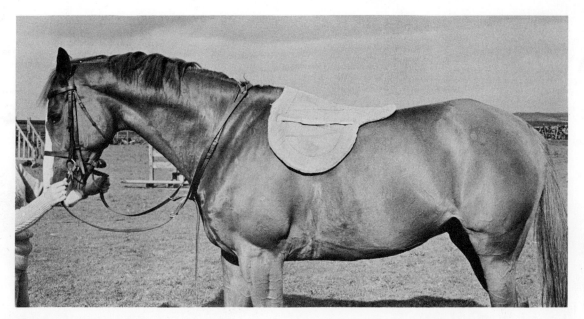

A numnah will make the saddle as comfortable as possible for the horse

regret spending money on good leather because it is safer and lasts longer. I have had a lot of success with buffalo hide. It is strong and will give a little when a horse tenses himself up as he goes over a fence. I find it especially worthwhile for the girth, and buffalo stirrup leathers are virtually unbreakable.

If you are dealing with children, the saddle must have safety bars for the stirrups to hang from, and the stirrups must have safety irons for the feet.

Check regularly to make sure that the safety bars are in perfect working order, so that the stirrups will slip off easily if there is an accident, and also see that the stirrup irons are not too large so that a child can slip a foot right through and become trapped.

To help make the saddle as comfortable as possible for the horse, put a numnah on his back first, and make sure that it is washed frequently. When a horse perspires a lot of salt comes out of his skin, and if you don't keep washing the numnah he will soon get saddle sore.

I use a breastplate to make completely sure that the saddle – and myself – stay in the right position. (See photograph on page 24.)

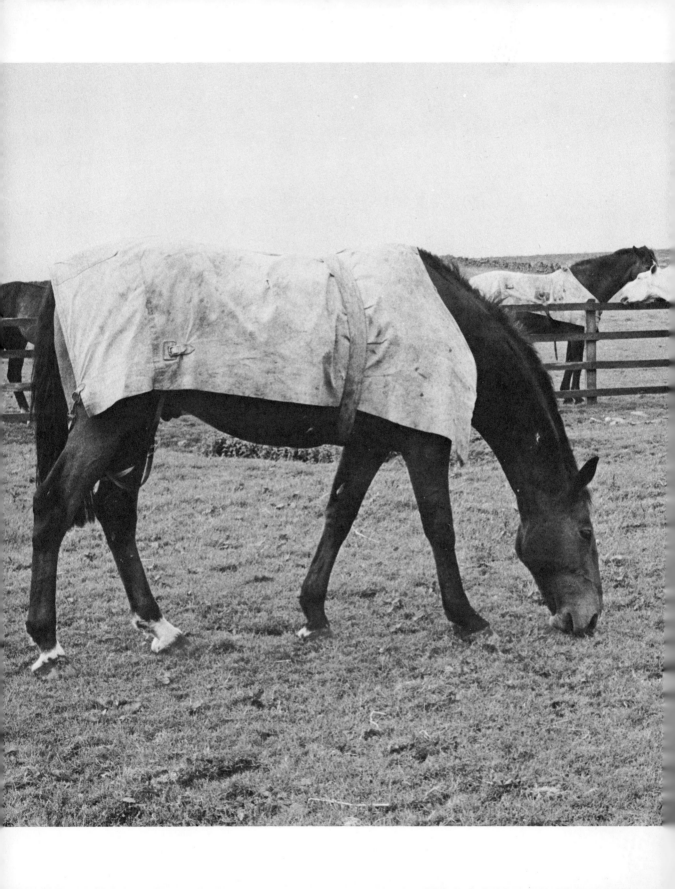

5 Horse and pony care

A labourer who worked on my father's building site bought a pony for his kids, and after a while he complained to me that the animal was losing weight and generally not well. When I asked what the pony was eating he said: 'Oh, I'm giving him as much bread and teacakes as he'll take!'

Some years ago a lot of very cheap Welsh ponies came on the market and many parents, anxious to give their kids a treat, snapped them up and tried to keep them in their back gardens. The outcome in many cases was tragic for there isn't enough grass in most back gardens to keep a horse or pony for five minutes.

I cannot remind you enough that if you want to keep a horse or pony seek expert advice first.

Livery stables can be a bit expensive so the best thing is to ask a local farmer if you can graze your horse or pony in his fields. The main problem is finding a farmer to help who is fairly close to your home, so that you don't have to make a long journey every time you want to visit your horse or pony.

Ideally, you should knock up a small shelter — nothing very complicated — so that the animal can dodge the worst of the weather in winter. Between April and October he will be quite happy roaming about the field without cover, but he should certainly be provided with a New Zealand rug — a wrap-around tarpaulin — in the winter months.

With the New Zealand rug he will cope with rain and frost because his thick winter coat will keep him warm enough. But if you are not using him a lot you must remove the New Zealand rug regularly (ideally once a day) to make sure he is not sore or losing weight.

If you keep your horse outside in winter be sure to protect him with a New Zealand rug

Parents should also be particularly watchful for the child who quickly loses that early rush of enthusiasm for the pony — the animal still needs looking after regularly.

Remember, too, that you cannot give your horse or pony a heavy day at weekends after leaving him in the field all week. He can stand any amount of work, but you must build up gradually.

Grass is the natural food for a horse and there is plenty of that about. He won't complain if you can only spend time with him at weekends and for the rest of the week leave him in the field with just grass.

He must always, however, have a supply of water. That is very important.

If you are going off pony-clubbing or show jumping your horse or pony will need something other than grass to help him cope with the extra work, but be careful not to overdo it. You will spend half your life picking yourself up off the floor if you over-feed him because he will get too frisky. You can easily get advice from your local feed merchant or talk things over with an old horseman.

In the winter he will certainly need some extra food to supplement the grass if he is left in the field all week; you can hang a haynet in his shelter and give him some concentrated foods.

The stabled horse

As an international rider I have a string of top-class horses and I have the assistance of grooms and my two sons in the stables, but I like nothing better than exercising the horses when I am not on tour.

On a typical day at my stables the horses are fed about eight o'clock in the morning. Some stables like starting at six, but I leave my horses another couple of hours because with con-

A horse's bed should be fit for you to sleep on. My horses have their beds made up with wood shavings and the floor is always well covered in case they want to lie down

stantly travelling to shows we often do not get home until nearly midnight and I reckon a horse wants a bit of time on his own.

Every horse is fed differently. For example, if he is a bit of a tiger he gets fed down but I insist that all our horses have a good supply of bran as this provides the roughage to keep their natural motion going, which the grass would do normally. It also stops them getting colic.

After the morning feed each stable is thoroughly cleaned out and the droppings removed. I use wood shavings for our horses' beds and make sure the floor is well covered in case they want to lie down.

Some prefer to make a horse's bed with wheat straw because it is easy to handle and gives good drainage, but I don't recommend using barley straw because it is prickly and irritates the horse. There are still others who use peat moss.

Always make sure that the bed is fit enough for *you* to sleep on, never mind the horse.

Feeding

Once we have worked out how much food each horse needs we try to spread it over about four

feeds a day. Some racehorse owners dish it out over as many as five feeds a day.

The horse has a small stomach and should not be overloaded. If you give him two big meals a day he will leave a lot, rather like you do when you have a big blow-out at lunch-time at Christmas and can't face another large meal for the rest of the day.

The more feeds you can spread it over the better. Left alone grazing in a field the horse does this naturally.

I like my horses without a lot of belly, fairly light, but with plenty of top on them. After years of experience I can quickly spot whether they are putting weight on or losing it (you can get quite a variation over only two or three days).

Exercise

If your horse is kept in a stable he must be taken out for at the very least half an hour's exercise each day, either ridden or just turned out into the paddock.

At home in Yorkshire the moors around my farm are ideal for exercising my horses, and every day we try to give each one of them about an hour's work.

I enjoy that part of the day when we exercise the horses and I make sure that it means something both to the animal and to myself. Even when I am just hacking in the countryside it is important I make it clear to him exactly what I want.

When I take a horse out of the stable first thing in the morning I start by putting his head round to my left toe and then to my right toe to make all his neck and spine supple and relaxed. Some horses just hang on the bridle like lumps of wood when they start work; by moving his head from side to side I am also telling him to listen and do as he is told.

All the time we are out I am feeling at him, not just sitting there looking at the birds and bees and enjoying the countryside. I concentrate and make sure that he thinks about what he is doing.

I might begin with a half-hour ride across the moors and follow this with fifteen minutes' circl-

Each morning when I take a horse out I start by turning his head first to the left toe and then to the right to make his neck and spine supple and relaxed. By doing that I'm also telling him to pay attention

ing, doing figure of eights, changing legs . . . all the things necessary to keep the horse supple and balanced. After that I will canter home and put him on the walking machine for twenty minutes to cool down. Then he receives a thorough grooming which can take anything up to an hour, has his rugs and bandages put on and is turned into a field until about five o'clock when he comes in to the stables for his tea-time feed.

Not many people turn them out into the field like that after exercise, but when I arrive at a showground anywhere in the world and turn four or five of my horses out into a paddock they straight away put their heads down and eat. If you did that with the run-of-the-mill show jumper he would gallop round and do something silly: normally he has no freedom because his owner is frightened to turn him out. I educate my horses by making sure they are turned out every day.

Sometimes a groom will take them out for a leisurely hack round the countryside once we get into a season, just to keep them fit and their muscles toned up.

A horse I am using on the circuit needs exer-

cise every day, but there is no point over-doing it. I don't want to jar him up or make him stale, I just need to make sure that he has a little variety in his life. If you were locked up in your school or office for seven days a week, six months of a year you would go potty, so it is important that — like you — the horse can get out and see different people and other things.

If one of my horses is not going just right, something is not fitting exactly into place, it can be like setting up a carburettor on a car when I go out with him.

I leave my horses in the field all winter because after being shut up and molly-coddled throughout the jumping season it is important that they should go back to nature. A holiday at grass, their natural food, gives the system a complete rest from artificial meals.

Grooming

To a horse or pony, good, regular grooming is very important. To the youngster with a pony of their own, grooming the animal is a vital part of building up a close relationship and, hopefully, a successful partnership. And to many more, being a groom at a top stable is a satisfying, if demanding job.

The horses that I keep in my stables and need to have in tip-top condition for the jumping circuit must have half- to three-quarters of an

29

Off to another show – one of my horses groomed and smartly dressed in his day rug and travelling bandages

chippings because a horse will not spend a penny on the journey if he thinks he is going to splash his legs. He doesn't realize the bandages he wears for travelling will protect him.

Eventually, when the wagon is fully loaded, work can begin on grooming the horses, washing their manes and tails and putting on their day rugs and travelling bandages, and this can take up to an hour for each horse.

During the show the horse must look like a million dollars when he goes into the ring to compete, with his mane and tail plaited to add the right finishing touch.

The equipment carried by my groom in her little box of tricks includes:

*A hoof pick for cleaning out the feet and hooking away stones and any other objects that get lodged there.

*Dandy brush for removing dirt and stains from the coats and mud off the legs, and anything else that might have stuck to the horse.

*Rubber curry comb, which is used with a circular motion to bring any grease to the surface.

*A body brush, which is a soft brush for finishing the job by removing scurf and dirt: again used with a circular motion so that it provides a massage.

*A metal curry comb to take grease out of the body brush as you use it.

*Cloth to give the horse a final rubbing over, which will remove any remaining dirt and add a nice shine to the coat.

If you leave your horse or pony in a field for a few days a lot of dirt and grease will gather in his coat, so when you take him out for exercise knock his mane over with a dandy brush to make sure it is laying properly, and then brush his back where the saddle sits otherwise he could easily become sore.

Then, when you have finished riding him, he must be thoroughly groomed before he goes back into the field; making sure that you brush out the sweat marks caused by the bridle, saddle blanket and girth.

Even if you do not have time to ride your horse or pony frequently still try to clean his feet

hour's grooming every day, but if you just have the one horse and keep him in a field you don't have to groom him every day if you cannot spare the time. (In any case, in winter horses and ponies kept at grass need the natural grease and dirt in their coats to protect them from the wet and cold.)

Forget about becoming a groom if you are a bit of a clock-watcher, for a groom at a top stable often has to work long, hard days, especially when a show is on.

A visit to a show usually means a long, tiring journey preceded by a great deal of preparation; on the day we set off my groom usually has to be up at six o'clock feeding the horses.

After that all the stables have to be mucked out and all the routine jobs done before she can pack the wagon with food and clothing for ourselves and the horses for a stay away covering maybe three or four days, or even longer.

It is so easy to overlook something when saddles, bridles, tendon boots, bandages for jumping and other vital pieces of equipment are being loaded.

When the back of the wagon has been thoroughly cleaned out we put down a bed of

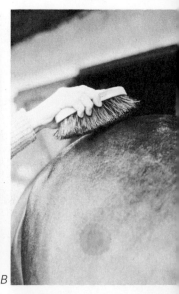

Inside the groom's box of tricks.
With this equipment she makes my
horses look their best when they
compete in the ring

A The hoof pick
B The dandy brush
C The rubber curry comb
D The soft body brush
E The soft body brush used in
   conjunction with a metal curry
   comb
F The final polish

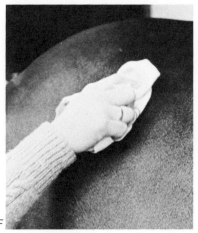

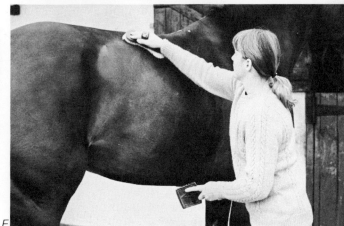

Oiling the feet with pure animal fat makes them grow well and strong. I believe this should be done every day, though many would not agree with that

out every day. If he has a stone wedged in a shoe he could quickly go lame.

Personally I believe that the feet should be oiled every day with pure animal fat so that they grow well and strong but I am aware that a lot of people will disagree with that advice, so talk it over carefully with an experienced horseman.

Also, clean the feet just before you ride in an event so that your horse will have every chance to get a good bite on the turf. If his feet are clogged up with mud – besides having extra weight – he could easily slide on a wet patch.

Shoeing

My horses are shod at least once a month, sometimes every three weeks, but if your horse is not doing a great deal of hard work you might stretch it to about six weeks, but never longer. It is essential that you go to a reliable black-smith.

A horse's foot grows twice as fast at the toe as it does at the heel and if it gets too long you will have a lot of tendon trouble.

I put an ordinary hacking shoe – the fullered shoe – on some of my jumpers; on others I use a broad aluminium shoe, particularly if the horse has a soft sole. The broad shoes are especially helpful if the horse has bruised his foot landing on a small piece of gravel or on a stone.

To help the horse that does not grow enough heel naturally we slip a plastic wedge into the heel to alter the angle of the horse's foot so that he can land and roll and move away without over-straining his tendons.

The fullered shoe has a groove on the side that goes to the ground in which the nail holes are placed and which provides a better foothold. But to give your horse or pony enough bite when he lands over a fence you should screw a jumping stud into each shoe, at the heel, and on the outside of the foot. Top-class riders often use two studs, but one is adequate.

When the studs are not needed plug the hole with cotton wool.

The worst time is just after a heavy shower when the ground is hard. Without studs your pony might easily fall through the fences under those conditions and things could become dangerous.

Studs are made in several different shapes and sizes: pointed and fairly narrow for when the ground is hard and bigger ones to help when it is soft. You do not need a stud, however,

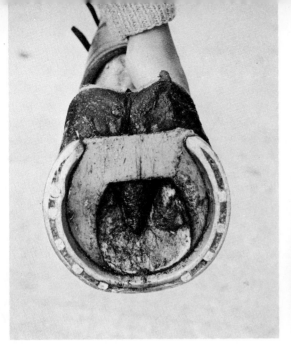

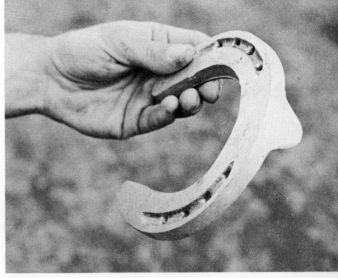

Above: *An ordinary hacking shoe – the fullered shoe – is fine for some jumpers*

Above right: *A broad aluminium shoe helps a horse with a soft sole*

Opposite: *A plastic wedge is used to help the horse that does not grow enough heel naturally*

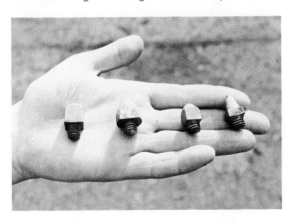

There is a stud for every occasion, to give your horse or pony a better footing on landing

One stud for each foot – outside heel – should be enough

when the going is really soft because the horse's feet will bed themselves down enough.

You should use studs mainly when you have a lot of grass on top and the ground is hard underneath and especially when there has just been a shower.

They always say that a horse has got not one but five hearts – the frog provides an additional heart in each foot. Apart from giving the horse a soft cushion to walk on, the frog, as the foot goes to the ground, pumps the blood back up through the legs.

6 What makes a good rider?

The ideal show jumping jockey – as I mentioned earlier – must have the balance of a ballerina. You cannot be in control of a horse without good balance, which simply means that you are sitting comfortably, just as you would if you were riding a cycle properly. Try to picture the correctly balanced rider and horse, going along at a canter, bouncing like a golf ball when it falls on firm ground.

You must always be relaxed on a horse, conveying the feeling to the animal that you are confident: if you do not feel too sure of yourself and nip him with your legs he will soon sense that something is wrong.

The more upright the rider sits the easier it is to maintain balance. I do not mean sit up stiffly like a tailor's dummy, but if your back is straight and you are sitting well down into the saddle you will feel naturally balanced.

Do not ride on short stirrups with your knees tucked up like a steeplechase jockey who has to lean on the horse's mouth to keep balanced. The only time I bend forward is when I am taking a fence and I sit on a horse feeling loose; really loose.

As you put your saddle on, you can obtain a quick guide to the right length for the stirrup by stretching out an arm and putting the fingertips on the buckle and the bottom of the stirrup iron just under the armpit. The bottom of the stirrup irons should touch the ankle bones when you sit in the saddle with your legs hanging fully downwards.

Viewed sideways, the rider sitting correctly on his horse looks very nearly straight from head to toe.

One of the most naturally balanced horses I've ever seen – Sportsman ridden by David Broome, seen here in the Grandstand Trophy at Hickstead, 1973

It must be a good idea to sit down in the saddle like the cowboys because they have to be naturally balanced to ride for hour after hour.

Basically your legs send the horse forward and your hands direct him and control his pace: if you and your horse are both correctly balanced you will need very little leg and he will respond to the lightest touch on the bridle.

The right saddle will enable you to grip the horse with the inside of the thighs, the knees and the calf muscles. The stirrup should be under the ball of the foot and though you need always to keep your legs firmly against the horse's side be careful not to get a feeling of tension into your legs for this would soon spread to the rest of the body.

I developed my balance as a youngster at gymkhanas, galloping about with no saddle and vaulting on and off my pony. The right balance will come only if you are prepared to work at it.

Riding with your feet out of the stirrups will improve your grip. Better still, ride bareback. That makes you grip firmly and do everything you want to naturally.

If you get out with your horse only at weekends, have a short session on him without a saddle. Then, maybe a little later, when you go for a ride, cross the stirrups over the top of the saddle for a spell. You must always be prepared to improvise in show jumping.

If you panic and crush your legs against the horse when your feet are out of the stirrups he will fly off through the bridle and you will soon have to loosen your grip.

Some instructors like to get novices used to riding with the feet out of the stirrups by having the horse on the lunge.

At first your legs will tire quickly riding without a saddle or with your feet out of the stirrups, but if you practise conscientiously you will soon improve.

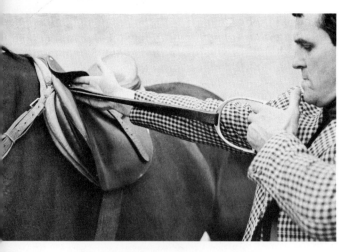

Above: *A guide to the right length for your stirrup — stretch out an arm and put the fingertips on the buckle and the bottom of the stirrup iron under the armpit*

Opposite: *To check the length is correct — when you sit on the horse the bottom of the stirrup iron should be level with the ankle*

Below: *The naturally balanced rider sits down in the saddle — like the cowboys — and viewed sideways looks very nearly upright from head to toe*

When you get a little more advanced, another useful exercise when riding with your feet out of the stirrups is to trot down a few cavalletti, dropping hands and reins at the same time. This will boost your confidence as well as improve your balance.

I hardly need remind you that the key to successful show jumping is having good balance, but to emphasize the point let me tell you about a couple of incidents when having good balance saved me during competitions.

I was riding Farmer's Boy in the puissance at the British Timken Show some years ago when my girth broke half-way through the round, but I managed to slide the saddle out and ride on without it to complete a clear round, including a jump over a 6ft 6in. fence.

On another occasion, a stirrup snapped when I was two or three strides off a bank in the Hickstead Derby. Caught out momentarily I had a fence down, but recovered to complete the course without any further mistakes.

Riding bareback will help you obtain the right balance and the correct grip with the legs. You grip the horse with the inside of the thighs, the knees and the calf muscles

With the arms hanging naturally down by your side, hold the reins with the first three fingers and the thumb

No doubt some of you will add small variations to what I have suggested here, but remember that being balanced also means being completely comfortable.

When you sit on your horse your arms should hang naturally down by your side, with the reins held between the three middle fingers and thumb. The forearms and reins will then make a straight line to the horse's mouth.

It is essential that you have light, sympathetic hands so that the horse will respond to the slightest touch on his bridle. A rider who grips the reins too tightly can easily spoil a horse's mouth.

The horse should then be balanced between the hands and the legs . . . the basis of all good riding.

With the legs applying an even pressure to drive my horse forward, I like to feel him with my hands and then when I go down to a jump it's like something boiling in my hands, waiting to explode.

Try dummy spurs if the horse doesn't pay enough attention

If dummy spurs do not work, try something a bit sharper. But don't wear spurs as a matter of course — only when the horse is not very bright

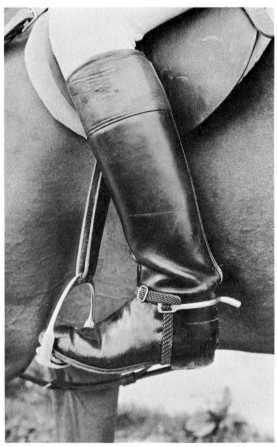

I have rarely seen a horse more naturally balanced and better on the bridle than Sportsman, ridden by David Broome. Obviously he is a dream to ride because he is always on the bridle, asking what the jockey wants of him next.

In my book, you should always have contact with your horse's mouth. I certainly don't agree with those foreign instructors who argue that a horse should be allowed to lead and flow on loosely. You must always have him between your legs and your hands.

Tied in with this are the different schools of thought on what is an ideal style. The Italians, for example, try to put the emphasis on getting the horse to flow freely with the jockey leaning forward as if following the horse. That is all right with fences up to about 4ft 6in., but when the jumps get bigger you really have to know what you are doing.

Peiro d'Inzeo rides very much like that, but his younger brother, Raimondo — on whom I have largely modelled my own style — always sits with the reins between his hands and the horse between his legs so that he can tell the horse where he is going. Raimondo's style, as I've mentioned before, takes nothing out of him, as evidenced by the fact that though he is well into his fifties he is still a top-class rider.

By contrast, the Germans like to tug and tow a horse about, making the rider doubly domineering. The Germans, to my way of thinking, are far too dictatorial to their horses; whereas the British will take a horse out in the morning for a bit of a gentle exercise, the Germans will take an animal out and annoy him for an hour.

If a horse doesn't listen to your leg enough, put on a pair of dummy spurs and if they do not work put on something a bit sharper. If you are

trotting on and put your leg to him he should automatically go away from that leg. If he leans on your leg you are lost because he is doing exactly the opposite of what you want him to do.

The good jockey should never let his horse go into a corner leading with the outside leg because this will make him unbalanced; though there are a good many top-class riders who do just shuffle round on the wrong leg. The horse should be shown early in his training how to change his leading leg.

If, as you approach a corner, he is leading with the wrong leg, pull him back to a trot and then apply the inside rein and the outside leg.

To keep him balanced between fences you will also need to work on adjusting the length of your horse's stride, but this of course can only be mastered through time, patience and experience.

An unorthodox style is fine so long as it works for you. Alan Oliver – seen here on Sweep competing in the Corrall Championship Stakes at the South of England Show, 1972 – adopted an unusual aerobatic style and was one of our leading show jumpers

It's not a bad idea for you to run and jump a low fence a couple of times yourself to help your understanding of the horse's problems: sometimes you will reach your take-off point with a clean, even stride, but other times you will have to do a little shuffle to even things up.

In simple terms, to shorten a stride you hold the horse up in front; and to lengthen a stride you drive him from the back.

You cannot begin show jumping until you know your horse, have him obedient and supple, and are handy with your aids. A horse who resists his jockey in the show ring is bound to bring trouble. He must be listening to you all the time so that when you put your legs to him he

goes forward, and if you catch hold of his reins he comes back. Without that kind of understanding you will soon be landing in the middle of the fences.

A horse must be taught how to be obedient from the start, and a jockey will not have full control until he can use the aids efficiently. There are two kinds of aids, natural and artificial. The natural aids are the jockey's body, legs, hands and voice — and the artificial aids include reins, whip and spurs.

Only by constantly repeating things can the right understanding between horse and rider be achieved.

I am presuming that you will have had a sound initial instruction in riding and can use the aids to dictate the pace and direction a horse must take. Also, that jockey and horse understand the four paces at which the horse moves — the walk, trot, canter and gallop.

Incidentally, a lot of people don't bother training their horse to go in reverse, but I believe this is important if the horse is to be fully obedient.

No two riders are alike and it does not matter whether you have an unorthodox style providing that it works for you, that you are consistent and the horse knows exactly what you are doing — and that the two of you have been married up properly. My good friend Alan Oliver used to have an unusual aerobatic style when he was a youngster, getting a fair distance out of his saddle as he went over a fence, and more recently the Australian rider Jeff McVean, has had success with a similar style, getting as much as three feet out of his saddle going over a fence.

Just as styles vary from jockey to jockey, so too does the time it takes to build up the perfect relationship with a horse.

People who go out and buy a horse and then enter a big class with him the day after are tempting disaster, because, with rare exceptions, a horse simply cannot know what the rider wants in that time. Creating an ideal relationship with a horse is, again, like a marriage — some folk court for ten years and others no more than a week.

For example, the first time I sat on Harvester at the Great Yorkshire I knew that we would get on together and three weeks later he was winning some of the biggest classes in the country.

It was the same with O'Malley. I first sat on him at the Great Yorkshire early in July 1972 and at the end of the same month we won the John Player Trophy, the British Grand Prix, at the Royal International Horse Show. He was my handwriting from the moment we met.

When I rode Alwin Schockemohle's horse, Donald Rex, in the World Championships I could almost make him talk we fitted so well together, and afterwards Alwin Schockemohle said he had never seen anything like it. The horse fitted right into me.

But obviously it is not always as simple as that. I've had a lot of horses that I had to persevere with, often getting close to giving up before they have come good. They all have something different about their characters, so you keep on with them for different reasons. Summertime was a desperate horse at one stage and would dump me on the floor in a couple of minutes, but he came good in the end.

The Australian Jeff McVean has proved successful with a similar style to Alan Oliver's. He is seen here on Claret en route to winning the King George V Gold Cup at the Royal International Horse Show, Wembley 1978

7 Schooling the show jumper

It is important not to expect too much too quickly from your horse when you start jumping with him. Take your time and build up gradually. The patience you show at this stage will always be fully repaid in the long run.

Poles on the ground

Open by putting a trotting pole on the ground and letting him walk over it a few times, making sure that he has enough rein to drop his head and see the pole and get a nice rounded back.

Then, one by one, add further poles until you have about half-a-dozen on the ground, parallel to each other about four feet apart for horses and three feet apart for ponies, and let him walk up and down them.

The idea is to improve the balance of the pair of you and have the horse concentrating, so that he is watching where he is putting his feet and also improving his agility and suppleness. It's like a cricketer when he goes to the nets. The horse must concentrate properly — he needs a good eye for the poles just as a cricketer needs a sharp eye for the ball.

This is where the experienced pony is invaluable in the way it can teach a novice jockey how to get the balance right.

After a time move the poles a little further apart and have him trot down them. Also give him a bit of variety by varying the path you take through the poles, going from corner to corner in a figure of eight as well as straight down the middle. He must never be allowed to become too content in his mind.

You bought him to be a jumper so there is nothing wrong with introducing him to a little

A dream horse in action — Donald Rex, with his regular partner the German international Alwin Schockemohle

Opposite: *Walking over a single pole on the ground*

Below: *Walking down poles*

Trotting down poles

Introducing the horse to his first jump

jump on the first day; say something like a small pole, starting with six inches and maybe edging it up to twelve, possibly eighteen inches high.

In the early days, play with your horse or pony for only fifteen or twenty minutes at a stretch and give him as much variety as possible. After he has been trotting over the poles and popping over a small jump, let him trot away from the poles for a bit before going back to them.

If you keep drilling a horse at the same thing you will soon make him bored.

Spare the time to play with him in this way for half-an-hour each day if you can and you will soon have him trotting down and clearing

fences as high as four feet; possibly after only a week. But also remember that if he trots to a fence and has a disaster lower it immediately. *Never persist with a disaster.* Show jumping is all about confidence, and you must make sure that he believes in what he is doing all the way along the line.

Cavalletti

When your horse is used to walking and then trotting over poles on the ground, introduce him to a cavalletti; a very useful piece of equipment for training, made by fixing a crossed stand to

A cavalletti

each end of a stout pole, forming an obstacle that can rapidly be changed to three different heights – 1ft, 1ft 6in. and 2ft.

Introduce him to a few cavalletti as you did the poles, first walking and then trotting along them. This way you will make him bend and buckle and become completely supple.

While the horse is trotting to things he will always have a leg on the floor for take-off. The trot, remember, is a pace of two time in which he advances by springing alternately from one diagonal pair of legs to the other.

Small fences

You will be surprised how fast your horse or pony progresses if you keep trotting him to a small single fence for a fortnight. He'll soon start to pick the job up and he can trot up to anything as much as four feet high.

On the days when you just take your horse out for a little exercise it is not a bad idea to let him trot up a line of poles on the ground as you go out and to trot down them on your return. This will keep his brain in touch with his feet.

Once he can cope with a vertical about three or four feet high, you can let him try a parallel, a hog's back and a triple.

The first parallel should be no more than a couple of feet wide, and now he will need to canter to the jump because the trot will not give him the speed to clear it and he could easily step on the back bar and turn over.

The canter, remember, is a pace of three time, with the sequence starting with the outside hind, followed by the outside diagonal and the inside fore.

Keep the canter controlled when you go to a fence. Too frequently you will see beginners going hell for leather the length of the paddock to take a jump and then they will tell you that whenever their horse sees a fence he runs away. He is not running away. He just thinks, 'Ah, poles, I must be quick to jump them.' This is why it is important to just trot to an obstacle in the beginning.

Because each horse is different, and a lot depends on the jockey's ability, it is not possible to say exactly how long it will take to graduate to a small vertical and from there to cantering to a parallel and so on. Personally, I tend to be a little impatient, but I am not recommending that you should be like that.

Never forget that it is the time you spend on him that makes a horse, and shortcuts can ruin him. The longer you spend working patiently with your horse the better it will be in the end for both of you.

A vertical

A parallel

A hog's back

A triple

If you took up to three weeks or a month trotting over poles on the ground, cavalletti and small vertical jumps before you started cantering to jumps you would be on the way to making a good horse because he would not want to rush a fence at any time and, just as important, he would learn to enjoy it.

Training plans

I do not believe in rigid training plans, though I imagine some orderly-minded people might prefer things thoroughly organized. I want to feel a horse as I'm going. When I take him out I do what I think he wants. If you decide he must have dressage one day, something else the next day and so on and so forth it will be like you landing home and knowing that you would be having fish and chips for tea on Monday, bacon and egg on Tuesday and baked beans on Wednesday. If you were aware of exactly what was going to happen each day of your life you would soon be fed up.

I don't know from week to week what I am going to do with a horse, though I bet the Germans would know a year ahead.

If a horse goes off I slip him back into the field for a week or a fortnight then bring him back. It's a feeling between my horses and myself and I suppose you have that only after a great deal of experience. You have got to feel how they are going.

To illustrate my point that you cannot judge all horses alike and that there is no point in having a rigid training plan, let me tell you about a five-year-old horse I bought in Dublin in the summer of 1978.

He was a freak and took to jumping fences almost immediately. He had been broken in when I shipped him over from Ireland but had done no jumping, and the day after he arrived at my farm he was doing the sort of things top international horses can do.

I just took him into the paddock and trotted him to some little poles and he quickly got better and better ... and in just over half-an-hour he was running down and clearing five feet as if he had been doing it all his life.

It was like discovering a Pele in a small Brazilian village. All I had to do was show him a fence. It didn't matter how he arrived at the fence he was naturally balanced and just jumped it.

It's sheer luck when you find a horse like that and he clearly gives the lie to all those people who claim that horses do not enjoy jumping.

Realizing that I had a freak on my hands — there's no other way to describe him — I determined not to make the mistake of over-facing him. Like any other horse fresh to jumping he began by walking and then trotting over poles on the ground and then carefully graduated to small fences and eventually was entered at a few small shows.

After playing with him when he first arrived he went into the field for several months until we had stopped rushing round the shows and had time to work with him.

Even though he had quickly and successfully tackled fences as high as five feet it would have been very wrong of me to start him off in competitions at anything higher than two feet, possibly 3ft 6in. because it would simply over-face him. He still had to learn his trade carefully so that when he went into the ring eventually he was relaxed and doing his job easily.

If I had kept hammering him down to big fences it would have put him off and soon he would have gone into a ring thinking, 'Oh, my God, another big fence to jump. I'm going to be hammered again.'

You must always be careful to avoid over-facing a horse, and the fact that I had a freak on my hands increased the danger of this happening.

I would expect that horse to be travelling on my wagon as my number 5 or number 6 horse after a couple of years and then he will gradually upgrade himself until he is my number 1.

It will be about four years before he is winning really good classes, for you will not find many horses under nine or ten winning top classes.

And if you succumb to temptation and rush a horse at the start of his jumping career, you will lose a lot of good years at the end.

First competitions

Before going off with your horse to his first small show, he will need to have had a look at a little parallel, a triple, a hog's back and maybe a small gate and a wall. He should also be able to handle a double. If needs be, throw a sack over a pole when you are working with him . . . anything to keep him alert.

There are plenty of shows run by riding schools where the fences are only two feet high, possibly three feet, and at these you can try your horse out in a clear round competition first.

Today it is easier than it has ever been to introduce a horse to show jumping; and once you have your horse popping nicely over the fences at home he is ready to try his luck at a small show where he will show you what further training he needs. If he tries to avoid or pulls up at a fence you should build something similar at home until he is used to it.

You can then graduate from small shows to the BSJA newcomer and Foxhunter competitions and slowly increase the height of his fences.

If possible, I like to introduce a horse to jumping in his four-year-old winter and then, the following spring, try him out at small shows for about a couple of months. After that I return him to the field for three months and bring him back the following winter for the indoor shows. That way, when he is turned out after a spell jumping he can digest all that he has learned.

If you have just one horse or pony, don't think you must start jumping with him in the winter. You can begin when you like because the little shows where he can have his first taste of competition are held all the year round.

From the point where you start walking and trotting your horse over poles, through trotting and then cantering to small fences, you could have him ready for a newcomers competition or even a Foxhunter event after about six to eight weeks.

Whenever you feel your horse is losing interest let him have a rest from show jumping. He might go for anything between three and six months without showing any staleness, but

when that happens put him in the field for three or four months. He will return a far better horse, having absorbed all that you have taught him and fully refreshed. And he will come back looking for work, having become bored in the field.

Discipline

A wayward young horse, like an undisciplined child, should be sharply reprimanded when he does wrong for he must always know who is in charge. If he does need the stick one, two, possibly three sharp raps across his hind quarters should be enough.

Never strike a horse about the head or in front of the saddle, and when he needs punishing do so immediately.

Also, remember to reward him just as quickly when he does well, whether you are out training with him or competing in the ring.

I do not wear spurs as a matter of course; only when the horse is not very bright and has to be sharpened up a bit. (See photograph on page 40.) It all depends on how sensitive your animal is, but if you have a horse on a really short martingale you must have a big, strong pair of spurs to keep him up to it.

Lungeing

I do not believe in training a horse on a lunge without a jockey in the saddle or in a loose school. As a horseman I fail to see what you can teach a horse standing on the ground that you cannot achieve sitting on his back. I must have a close relationship with a horse if we are to succeed, and being apart from him won't achieve that.

Also, when a horse is on a lunge there is a serious risk of him twisting his joints and harming himself if he gets frisky and starts acting the fool. You will see a lot of horses with wind gall — a swelling at the back of the tendons on the hind legs — caused by having them on a lunge.

It seems to me that if you teach a horse to jump while you are off his back you have then to teach him all over again when you get back on him. I also believe that lungeing is a lazy way to teach a horse.

Loose Schooling

Loose schooling is very much a thing of the past and was really designed for middling-bad riders. The idea is to build a course round the edge of a reasonably tight enclosure so that the trainer can keep control and to have the horse gallop round on his own so that he feels free about his head. This is all right if you follow the Italian style of letting the horse do most of the leading, but not if you wish to always be in charge of the horse.

The danger with a horse that has been loose-schooled is that he is liable to jump out of your paddock because he is used to jumping on his own. But a horse that has always been ridden to fences can be turned into a field and would never make an attempt to escape, even if surrounded by a fence only 18 inches high.

The importance of variety

Remember that a horse should always have variety in his training. If you had just four fences on

The horse at take-off. Now there is nothing you can do but keep your balance – anything else would only hinder the horse. Bill Steinkraus (USA) on Fleet Apple at Hickstead, 1971

your place and took him over them day after day and week after week he would soon become sick of them. Vary the obstacles and set him different little problems as much as you are able.

Hints for the rider

When you take your horse to a fence he will decide the point where you take off ... at least until the fence is about 4ft 6in. high.

I have little doubt that some novice riders will be tempted to try to lift the head of their horse or pony as they approach a fence, but if you think for a moment about your weight compared with the weight of the animal, you will soon realize how silly that would be. Also – and more important – unless a rider knows exactly what he is doing it is extremely dangerous to try to pick a horse up going to a fence. A youngster could easily cause serious damage to the pony's mouth.

You should let a horse have his head approaching a jump so that he can stretch his neck out, curve his back into the correct bascule, and flow through the air.

From the moment I start walking a horse over trotting poles I let him drop his head so that he can weigh up the situation. I'm not suggesting that you should throw the reins away; just ease your contact a little so that he has the freedom to look and is not more concerned about you holding on to his mouth.

So that you are constantly building up his confidence to measure a fence and decide the take-off point himself make sure that you lower the fence whenever he has a disaster in training.

Your horse must first be bouncing to the fence like a golf ball: in other words completely balanced. Then, so that he can measure things up, let him lower his head two strides out and at

Can you spot the deliberate mistake in this picture? *The rider, having removed a pole to give the horse variety, has forgotten to take the spare cups off the front wings. Cups left on in this way can cause serious harm to a horse or pony*

the same time tighten you legs to encourage him to go forward. If he's a good horse, when he sees the fence he will come back on his own, before throwing himself into the air, snapping his knees up in front and clearing the object in a perfect arc.

When he snaps his legs back you must keep your balance for there is nothing you can then do to help him jump. At that stage you can only hinder him and the less you do that the better.

Only when a horse is really in trouble do I catch hold and tell him to pay attention as we get close to a fence, but that is not something I would encourage youngsters to try because they can cause so much harm.

The height of the fence will give you a guide to the take-off point for your horse or pony. For example, if the fence if about four feet high, he will take off betweeen five and six feet in front of it: something between one and one-and-a-half times the height of the fence. He will then land about the same distance beyond the fence.

Once you get above 4ft 6in. the jockey has to decide on the take-off point: the higher the fence the more precise the rider must be; and the stronger the leg he will need to put to the horse two strides out. By the time the rider has started going for fences that high he or she should have acquired a delicate enough touch with their hands so that they can pick the horse up without harming his mouth.

If a horse runs too deeply into a fence the jockey will have to pick him up with a very careful feel at the bit, but you can only manage that with many miles on the clock of experience.

Finally a word of warning! When you are out training your horse, if you re-arrange the poles make sure you never leave spare cups fixed into the wings because they can cut a horse's legs very badly.

8 Competing at shows

There is little to match the thrill of setting off to your first show with your own horse or pony.

As I mentioned earlier, there are plenty of unaffiliated shows (not run by the British Show Jumping Association) that have fences and course builders of a good standard, and where the beginner can obtain the right experience in a show ring. Usually they start with a clear round competition where there is no jump-off and every competitor receives a rosette for completing a clear round.

Then, when you have some experience, you will be able to move on to BSJA events like the Newcomers and Foxhunter, where the competition is slightly more advanced but equally as encouraging to the novice.

Ideally, you will take your horse to a show in a small trailer, but that may be easier said than done for many of you, and the hire of a wagon can prove expensive.

I still have horses ridden to local shows from my farm in Yorkshire, and there is nothing to stop you hacking to a show, five, six, seven, even ten miles away from your home.

The old stars of show jumping, like Ted Williams and Don Beard who appeared in my television series, used to travel long distances to events by train; often hacking several miles to the local station and then having to walk the horse across London to change trains. Remember, too, that the old farmers years ago thought nothing of riding ten miles to a meet and then, after hunting all day, riding another ten miles home.

By the way, walk (don't gallop) down the road to a show, and your horse won't need his usual

They don't come any better than Ted Williams, seen here riding Rival at Hickstead in 1968. Inside the ring Ted could tackle just about any height but he never warmed up with anything big outside

53

exercise on the morning of the show. You will have to take some dinner-time feed for him in a sack.

Be sure to arrive on the showground in plenty of time so that you can check your entries and collect your numbers without a panic. I always aim to land at a show at least an hour-and-a-half before my first class and I like my horses, with their saddles and bridles on, to be out of the wagon and walking an hour before their class.

I usually let one of my girls sit on the horse and trail about the showground so that he gets used to the atmosphere and settles down — and that goes for my old horses as well. It's what I call mooching about.

Ten horses before I am due in the ring I get up on my horse to warm him up with some small parallels — nothing very high, about three feet, depending on how he's going — and usually finishing up with a decent size vertical about 4ft 9in. to 5ft, and then another little parallel. After that I like to move straight into the ring.

That is enough to make one of my horses supple and limbered up and ready to go like an athlete with his adrenalin flowing. But, of course, no two horses are alike.

If your horse or pony is a little bit on the fiery side and tends to become over-excited the moment he senses he is due in the ring, you are better off trying to kid him by warming up an hour early and then letting him go cold. The only danger is that by entering the ring cold you are taking a chance at the first fence.

Some like to put their horse on a lunge and let it run round in circles a couple of hours before an event, but that is definitely not my scene. I was always taught that if you are going to give instructions give them from the office — and that means you should be sitting on the horse to do anything with him.

Youngsters often wrongly warm their ponies up an hour before their event is due and they go on jumping and jumping so that by the time the animal enters the ring he is too damn tired to compete properly. All that is needed is to pop him over a little fence two or three times.

The Americans surprise me when they give their horses a fair bit of jumping before an event: often warming up over fences higher than those they will be meeting in the ring. I could never agree with that because if you have to teach a horse how to jump when you arrive at a show he should never be there.

I reckon my horses know how to jump before I set off so that all they require is a little limbering up just before they go in the ring. That great old trouper, Ted Williams (remember him on Pegasus), never jumped anything big outside a ring.

Several riders give themselves trouble by getting over-anxious. After their horse has, maybe, jumped a couple of practice fences well, they become keyed up and instead of leaving well alone they keep practising and practising until the horse is tired.

Then there is the horse that knocks over a couple of fences in the collecting ring, causing the jockey to become over-anxious and keep on practising in the hope of putting things right in time. There is no way you can improve a horse immediately like that. You are far better off leaving him alone until you go into the ring.

Fortunately nerves never bothered me when I was a youngster, but a good many are not so lucky and for some it is a very real problem.

A lot of riders do not help themselves by going round saying, 'Oh, so and so is here . . . ' and 'Have you seen so and so . . .? ' until they have talked themselves into trouble, and out of confidence. Forget the other competitors and concentrate only on jumping a clear round yourself.

Also parents can put a lot of pressure on children when they build them up in front of others, boasting that their Lizzie is better than so and so . . . and what a wonderful new pony they have . . . and how hard their child has worked to get the animal ready. Things then become even worse when the pony has a fence down and the parent becomes so worked up they pull the child off the pony and give them a spanking.

I must confess that when my two lads started jumping I — like a lot of parents — was over-anxious, until I remembered that that is a sure way to put children off. There is no substitute for miles on the clock.

In the beginning, I drilled them far too much, constantly telling them to do one thing and then another. But until youngsters have experience and have made a few mistakes themselves they cannot really understand what you are talking about.

At one stage my son Robert had a craze for going into corners and doing complete circles ... then wondering why he had picked up faults when he had not stopped. You must ride straight from fence to fence.

It is essential that novices — young and old — concentrate at the start on trying to achieve clear rounds. I have often heard kids who have just knocked four fences down say, 'Oh, but I had the fastest time!' They would have been a lot better with a slower time and a clear round. Putting too much emphasis on racing against the clock too early can ruin rider and horse.

If you want to keep improving, concentrate on precision in your riding. I go to every fence trying above all to be precise in everything I do for, if you don't have precision at the end of the day you don't have a jumper.

If a child is having clear rounds it doesn't matter if he or she is being beaten in the jump offs: that will come with experience as the competitor learns how to cut little bits off corners and, maybe, move a shade faster to the first fence.

I make it a rule to hand my horse over to the groom the moment I leave the ring so that I am not tempted to scold him if he has taken a liberty during the round.

If you have a disaster remember that there is another day and try not to lose heart too easily. Parents, particularly, should make sure that children reward their ponies with a lump of sugar whether a round has been good, bad or indifferent.

When you have an unhappy round sit and think about it for a bit and you will soon realize what went wrong. Much better to do that than lose your temper and tug at the horse's mouth, kick him with your spurs and generally make a fool of yourself by causing a scene.

Many children also forget to dismount when they have finished a round so that their pony can have a rest before he goes in the ring again, maybe for a jump off. That is important.

Riders should always be correct and polite to judges. Of course some judges shout at children when they should not and, like any other human being, they make mistakes — but that is no excuse for bad behaviour by competitors.

Always be ready for your turn in the ring and do not waste time when called by the collecting ring steward. On the other hand, don't get excited and rush into the ring and start before the bell. I've seen youngsters do that a few times.

If you knock down either of the starting posts you will be disqualified and the same goes for the finishing gate, so when you have cleared the last fence don't think, 'Thank heaven, I've finished,' and then let your pony wander all over the place.

On the odd occasions when you have a disaster make sure you hold on to your horse: if he gallops off and leaves the ring without you that will also lead to disqualification.

At shows run by the BSJA, you will see association stewards maintaining a close watch for things like ill-treatment of horses, illegal equipment and animals that might be lame. You should never forget they are there for your benefit, so be as helpful as you can.

I have found the BSJA stewards particularly good with children, usually taking them on one side when they have done wrong and offering a friendly word of warning.

After the show make sure your horse is well cooled off. Let him have a graze and eat a bit of grass while you rub him down and put his travelling bandages and rugs on. If your horse is perspiring when you put him in the trailer he will perspire all the more on the journey. It is important that you spend a bit of time with him at this stage of the day.

And if you are walking him home never overlook taking out his jumping studs before you set off.

9 All about courses

Before each event the course builder will display a plan of his course in or near the collecting ring. (The direction the course takes is marked with arrows, and the plan also tells you the distance between the start and finish and the time allowed.) Study it thoroughly and then walk the course along exactly the same line that you will follow when you jump it.

Take no notice of other competitors who amble haphazardly round the ring, talking and joking while walking the course — every moment you spend paying attention to detail at this stage will be amply rewarded later.

As you walk round, check on whether the course is tricky or trappy and long or short so that you can give your horse the best possible guidance.

Note the construction of the jumps, whether they be verticals, triple bars or hog's backs, and work out how one fence relates to another, pacing out the distance between them carefully.

The average stride of a horse when galloping in competition is approximately twelve feet and that of a pony nine feet: though not surprisingly this varies from horse to horse.

Under international rules, the distance between related fences in a combination must not exceed 39ft 4in. It is important that you work out the yardage between fences to see whether you will need to shorten or lengthen your stride.

Take, for example, a one-stride double combination; where the horse takes one stride between landing and taking off again.

Assuming that the horse lands 6 feet clear of the first obstacle and needs to take off 6 feet in front of the next fence, the ideal distance between the two jumps would be 24 feet (8 yards).

Ted Williams successfully tackles the Hickstead bank on Carnaval during the British Jumping Derby, 1968

To test the rider, a course builder varies the distance between fences in a combination: so that if you have 9 yards between obstacles, as sometimes happens, the horse needs to take a very big stride, and if there is only 7½ yards it will be a very short stride — unless, of course, you are on a pony.

In combinations I measure from the highest point of the jump at the first obstacle to the highest point at the next obstacle.

Sometimes the difference between jumps at a one-stride double is 10 yards — and that is the maximum he can reach.

Life was a lot more simple when I started riding. Courses in those days usually consisted of three fences up one side of the ring, three down the other and a triple down the middle. Also I had a horse that went on a very short stride: it didn't matter where the fences were placed I could just fiddle my way round.

Course building has gone through a very complicated era, but thank heaven it is coming back to where it should be. One fellow used to put as many as seventeen fences in his courses, making it far too complex. That isn't show jumping. It's a marathon designed to wear the horse out and make him sick of jumping.

I reckon that ten fences should be plenty; if a course builder cannot sort them out with ten fences then he should give up.

People go to a show to see good sport and a spectacle; horses and riders can provide that only if they are given a reasonable challenge over a well-designed course. Too often in recent years the battle of wits between the course builder and the rider and horse has got out of hand, and I'm convinced that World Championship and Olympic courses have now come very close to cruelty.

At the end of the day the careful and obedient horse should come through if a course has been

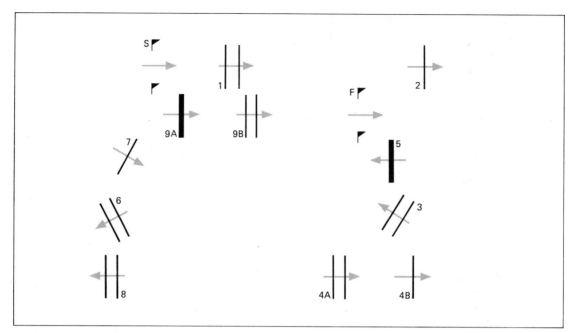

Table 'A4' Speed 328 Y.P.M.

Distance	437 yards		Jump off fences	
Time allowed	1.20 (80 secs)		Distance	
Time limit	2.40 (160 secs)		Time allowed	
			Time limit	

The plan of the course, displayed near the collecting ring, should be studied carefully

built fairly, but in the past fences and obstacles grew steadily wider and longer to get a result until we reached a point where only freak horses could succeed. Fortunately in Britain that kind of course has now been curbed.

When I talk about a freak horse in this context I mean the biggest athlete ... horses like Merely-a-Monarch, who could jump 3 feet wider and make 6 feet more ground in a combination than just about any other horse. Sunsalve was another freak.

Courses should be built for the middle-of-the-road horse who has a lot of ability but cannot cope with a big combination built on a long stride.

As I write this there is not really a good horse anywhere in the world because they have been frightened off by being constantly asked to go down to oxers (big spreads) and combinations that have been far too big. A horse that crashes into one of these huge fences never approaches it as bravely again.

Alan Oliver is an ideal course builder in my book. Using the experience he gained through many years as a top-class rider, he can create a course six to nine inches lower than many other course builders and still get the same result. He is able to do this because he has travelled round a lot of showgrounds and he knows the jockeys and horses thoroughly. Consequently, it is now second nature to him to build what appear to be nice, easy fences but which will often catch riders out.

I have returned from shows where Alan has been the course builder with my horses still fairly fresh and ready for another weeks' jumping, and I have been to other shows where the fences have been far too large and have left my horses physical wrecks.

There are basically four different types of fence in show jumping: a vertical or upright; a parallel or oxer; a staircase; and a hog's back.

The most common mistake youngsters make with the parallel is trying to jump the back bar instead of the front.

With the triple, or staircase, you need to get in a little bit closer to the bottom bar to give you a chance with the back bar, and you should always aim for the centre.

I tend to treat the hog's back — one of our oldest fences — a bit like I do a triple bar, getting in fairly close so that the horse can have a good chance of clearing the back pole.

The construction of a fence affects the chances of horse and rider just as much as its size.

It is very important to walk round the course before the event paying especial attention to every detail

In recent years some fences in World Championship and Olympic courses have come very close to cruelty. In this shot from the television series Alan Oliver has re-created an enormous fence to show the problems faced by competitors in the Mexico Olympic Games

In my television series, Alan Oliver recalls how a talk years ago with some steeplechase jockeys influenced his thinking on the way jumps should be constructed. Grand National fences used to be very hard and very severe; but after rightly pointing out that a horse is inclined to look at the bottom of a fence before taking off, the steeplechase men had their life made a little easier by the placing of kicking boards across the bottom of the jumps.

As it nears a fence a horse will lower its head and decide on a take-off point by looking at the groundline, or bottom of the fence. A horse can be deceived, therefore, by putting in a false groundline with boards or bushes standing behind the line of the poles. A fence with only one, maybe two poles and no obvious ground-line will also give a horse problems. These then become rider's problems and are good for sorting out the men from the boys.

To my way of thinking, it is better for course builders to use false ground lines to sort competitors out than to construct enormous fences. That way, at least, would encourage obedience

A board (or bushes) behind the front line of poles provides a false groundline

in an animal and good horsemanship in a jockey. On the other hand, I can understand why Alan Oliver argues that many average competitors and horses need well-constructed fences with clearly defined groundlines to encourage them to jump.

A horse can cope with height much easier than it can manage width in a jump and I firmly believe that no parallel should be built wider than its own height. The opposite has been the case far too often in recent years, giving horses back troubles that you never heard of when I started jumping.

I am pleased to see the practice of using heavy poles like small trees has now been stopped, but it's no wonder that with much bigger fences and a far busier and longer season the jumping life of a horse has been reduced quite a bit.

I would also like to see more jumps resembling things you see in real life; like stiles and road

Sally Mapleson coming to grief at the Hickstead Derby bank

closed signs. Also, poles should topple more easily than they do at present. The cups could be a little shallower for a start, and when a horse goes down to a brick wall and hits it the bricks should not be so large and heavy they can hardly fall off.

All credit to the British Show Jumping Association who realized a few years ago that poles and bricks were becoming too heavy. Now things have been pulled back to a more sensible level horses are getting brave again.

It is much better when fences are lighter and have a bit less filling. There could also be fewer fences in some rings with those that are left constructed in such a way to make every one of them count. I have jumped in competitions where there have been five or six fences that could not be knocked over, so they might just as well have been left out.

I fully appreciate the need for show jumping to provide a spectacle for the spectator, but hav-

ing jumped all over the world I am still not totally convinced that we need the huge Derby banks and devil's dykes.

I have also got reservations about parallels with privet hedges growing in between the poles, especially when they are combined with certain other fences.

At Hickstead, for example, a horse is asked to jump an Irish bank, where he is encouraged to land on the bank and then, two fences later, he meets a privet hedge growing between parallel bars. Not realizing that the hedge is soft many horses try to put their feet on top of it like they did the bank. The privet hedge also gives a false groundline to further confuse the horse.

In my book these things are gimmicks; not proper show jumping. It's getting round to three-day eventing.

Alan Oliver believes that natural obstacles like banks are all right for the English and Hamburg Derbies. but they should be used only in such events. He also thinks that the devil's dyke is fair in a speed competition or a Derby, providing it is not too high. The trouble is that more and more permanent grounds in England are copying them and suddenly they are no longer novelties.

I have had two horses fall off the top of the Derby bank at Hickstead. The year after, each stopped at the top of the bank and stood shaking their heads as if to say, 'No thanks'; which certainly disproves Prince Phillip's suggestion that a horse has no brains.

The Derbies, of course, have become great spectacles and I agree we can stand some of these fences in them, but it should go no further than that.

The good course builder will design this challenge only according to the standard of the entries on the day.

He must also bear in mind the need to keep to the time-table, so, for example, if he has thirty entries he will build a course that will produce approximately five clear rounds. It would be very boring for spectators if he built a course that produced clear round after clear round. So the course builder must weigh up very carefully the condition of the ground and the entries.

At my farm I have a water jump about 9 feet wide (it is not too difficult to construct a water jump yourself) and I use it to train my international horses who have to clear up to 16 feet over water in competition. In practice I get them to take the jump with several feet to spare to build up their confidence. Also, a horse would soon get tired if coached constantly over the international distance.

Taking the water jump on Salvador during the Nations Cup, subsequently won by the British team, Hickstead 1975

One of my favourite horses and one of my favourite events – on Graff in a puissance event

The water jump is very much a rider's problem, and many jockeys forget that a horse needs height to take it properly. They fly across the arena and give the horse problems when he has to slow up to put himself right for the jump. The ideal water-jumper can cope from five strides out.

Providing the horse gains enough height a water jump should provide no problem. The Germans are particularly good at it, partly because the German horses (unlike their English counterparts) never get turned into the field, so they rarely see a heavy shower or puddles and consequently they are frightened to death of water.

To help a horse find the right take-off point for the water jump Alan Oliver builds small rustic walls in front of them.

Top riders keep horses specially for speed events: when courses are designed with sharp turns and fences at difficult angles and the rider with the best-schooled horse usually comes out on top.

The trouble is, a lot of good young horses are spoiled by speed events for if you keep rushing a horse at fences when he is young he will become totally confused. The emphasis must be put on precision jumping at the start, and I believe that a horse should have at least two years' jumping before catching sight of a clock.

If you start racing him too early he will want to go faster and faster, and every time he enters a ring he will want to gallop round everything. Introducing a horse too early to speed classes also reduces his obedience.

I believe that no novice class, Foxhunter event or Grade C competition should be decided by the clock.

One of my favourite events is the Puissance where the aim is to test the explosiveness of a horse by putting the fences progressively higher. You need to be very precise to succeed in this competition and I have had a fair amount of success because I am a big, powerful jockey and I can hold a horse and get that little bit extra out of him. But you will have to be fairly experienced before you try this one.

10 The way ahead

The first time I travelled abroad with an international team was back in 1958 when I went to Dublin with Farmer's Boy. It was also the first time I had been out of England, and I was frightened to death and utterly lost because I knew no one.

I jumped a clear and four to help us win the Nations Cup and I was third in the Grand Prix and third in the Irish Championship. I also had to borrow a dinner suit that wasn't my size for official functions and I had to be sewn into it each time I went out.

The press had a bit of a swing at the British selectors for going to such an important show with a team that included a bricklayer (myself), a farmer, a housewife and an ex-steeplechase jockey. Thank heaven attitudes to international teams have changed a lot since then ... the problem now is that the courses they build for events like the World Championship and the Olympic Games have got out of hand.

At the Montreal Olympics the obstacles were far too big and dangerous for both horse and rider and many of the horses that competed in Montreal were not jumping a couple of years later. Had they not taken part in those Games they would still have been jumping today.

The organizers of these events are building fences that are far too high and wide. Horses should not be constantly asked to do the impossible. They must be kept within themselves.

When a soccer player from the Football League goes to the World Cup he is not suddenly confronted with a pitch twice the size he normally plays on; and a cricketer called up for a Test match does not expect the ball to come hurtling at him any faster than it does in a county match. The cricketer and footballer are not annihilated like a horse is if they do not get things right.

Why then should show jumpers be expected to face fences in the World Championship and Olympic Games that are far higher and wider than anything they meet elsewhere? The trouble is the organizers think to themselves: *'Ah, World Championship! We must build everything two feet higher and two feet wider'.*

They have got to be pulled back to a sensible level, with less material in the fences and lighter poles so that if a horse touches them they fall down and that's the end of the day. If not, they will go to the well once too often.

Show jumping has come a long way since the days of Harry Llewellyn and I have no fears for the future of the sport.

It is at its best indoors because then they cannot build big, long courses with fifteen and sixteen fences and it becomes a much sharper spectacle for the public. I also like indoor shows for the way the crowd is on top of you.

There is still a fair bit of hypocrisy over professional riders, but I reckon that anyone who goes show jumping more than a couple of days a week must be a professional.

If prize money is increased then competition will also go on improving. Wimbledon today is twice the spectacle it was ten years ago because of the introduction of professionals, and the same thing will happen in show jumping.

Professionalism has already improved the standard of riding in England to such an extent that today any one out of forty horses can win a class, and when I started it was any one out of ten.

There is nothing better than keen competition. I would rather see place money cut down and the plum at the top increased to stop those people who are content just to ride for place money.

I can only see show jumping spreading, and already many people are talking about it as they used to talk about soccer.

The Olympic Games should be thrown open to professionals, though not for prize money. They should continue to reward competitors with gold, silver and bronze medals, but if someone like Muhammad Ali wanted to enter the boxing championships and fight over three rounds he should be allowed to do so. That way we would find the true champion of the world at every sport.

There are still a number of things we can do to improve show jumping. For example, I would like to see bookies going more to events. Also, some of my fellow competitors could help spread and improve our image by being a bit more co-operative with interviews and things. But I can feel only optimism about the future because in the main the organizers are now very entertainment-minded.

Interviewing Capt. Mark Phillips for the television series